COMBAT SPORTS

# JUDO

## Paul Mason

SEA-TO-SEA

*Mankato Collingwood London*

This edition first published in 2011 by
Sea-to-Sea Publications
Distributed by Black Rabbit Books
P.O. Box 3263, Mankato, Minnesota 56002

Printed in China, Dongguan

Library of Congress Cataloging-in-Publication Data

Mason, Paul, 1967-
  Judo / Paul Mason.
    p. cm. -- (Combat sports)
  Includes index.
  ISBN 978-1-59771-274-3 (library binding)
  1. Judo--Juvenile literature. I. Title.
  GV1114.M3727 2011
  796.815'2--dc22
                              2009051536

9 8 7 6 5 4 3 2

Published by arrangement with the Watts Publishing Group Ltd, London.


Series editor: Adrian Cole
Art director: Jonathan Hair
Design: Big Blu
Cover design: Peter Scoulding
Picture research: Luped Picture Research


Acknowledgments:

Concord / WB / Album / AKG p29. United Artists / Album / AKG p19. Andrzej Gorzkowski / Alamy p20. Associated Press
pps 1, 22, 25. ABC UK / Aquarius p9. David Finch www.judophotos.com pps 8, 10, 11, 14, 16, 17, 21, 26, 28.
CourtesyofIceAssociatesLtd p23. M.E. Mulder / Shutterstock p18. The Kobal Collection p7, 15. Mary Evans Picture Library
p12. ITAR-TASS / Rex Features p4. The Ronald Grant Archive p5. Topfoto p13. Roger-Viollet / TopFoto p6.
Every attempt has been made to clear copyright. Should there be any inadvertent omission please apply to the
publisher for rectification.

March 2010
RD/6000006414/002

# CONTENTS

# INTRODUCING JUDO

What links Storm from the *X-Men* movies with the Russian leader Vladimir Putin? Don't know? The answer is...judo!

Judo is a competitive sport, and a way of defending yourself against a stronger attacker. In fact, judo was invented by someone who got sick of being bullied by bigger kids at school!

## JUDO UP IN LIGHTS

How does judo link together the two people mentioned in the first paragraph?

* In *X-Men 3*, Storm's stunt double was a judo black belt.
* Vladimir Putin is also a judo black belt.

*Vladimir Putin throws his opponent to the mat.*

## Competitive Judo

Judo fighters—called judoka—have been taking part in competitions ever since judo was invented. Some of the great champions have become TV and movie stars, and even comic-strip characters.

Storm (left) had the judo black belt Angela Uyeda as her stunt double.

## Judo for Self-Defense

Judo experts use timing and skill to throw their opponents to the ground. Even someone much bigger can be tackled using judo, so it is perfect for self-defense.

"A contestant shall be deemed to have been defeated when from any cause or causes he may become unconscious."

*Judo can be a tough sport, as you might guess from this extract of the original Kano Judo Contest Rules.*

# THE ORIGINS OF JUDO

Judo began in Japan just over 125 years ago. Its founder, Jigoro Kano (1860–1938), first became interested in combat sports when he was bullied at school.

## Kodokan Judo School

Jigoro Kano wanted to improve Japan's most popular fighting style, ju-jitsu. He developed a style that allowed a smaller person to defeat a bigger one. It was taught at his Kodokan Judo School in Tokyo.

*Jigoro Kano was an expert ju-jitsu fighter who went on to invent judo's first techniques. Here he is demonstrating a shoulder lock in 1935.*

## Battle between the Schools

In 1886, Kodokan judo fighters entered a competition with the Totsuka, the most famous ju-jitsu school. Two of the 15 fights were ties. The other 13 were won by Kodokan judo fighters.

Within two years, the Tokyo police had begun training all officers in judo. The spread of judo had begun.

"In those days, contests were extremely rough.... Thus, whenever I [went to one], I invariably bade farewell to my parents, since I had no assurance that I should ever return alive."

*Sakujiro Yokoyama, one of the first-ever judo experts, describes preparing for early competitions.*

*Susumu Fujita starred in the Japanese movie* Sanshiro Sugata *in 1943, which is set during the early days of judo. The story is so popular that the movie has been remade five times.*

# THE GENTLE WAY

The word "judo" is often translated as "the gentle way"—
even though you win contests by slamming an opponent
to the floor or by pinning them down.

### Skill not Strength

Judo techniques do not rely on strength alone. Instead, judoka use
technique and timing to defeat their opponents. For example, it is
much easier to step aside and trip an attacker than to push the attacker
backward. Judoka would always choose a trip instead of a push.

*Successful judo
throws rely on the
skill of breaking
an opponent's
balance, which is
called* kuzushi.

## Learning how to Fall

Judo is "gentle" because throws can be performed at full power without harming an opponent—as long as they know how to fall safely. This is why the first thing new judoka learn is *ukemi*, the art of falling.

## Women in Judo

It was because judo relies on skill rather than strength that in the early 1900s, it became a popular way for women to defend themselves. Then in the 1960s, Honor Blackman showed off her judo moves in the British TV show, *The Avengers*. It was a big hit, and Blackman went on to play the high-kicking Pussy Galore in the James Bond movie *Goldfinger*.

Honor Blackman shows off her judo skills playing Catherine Gale in The Avengers (1962).

# TOP 10 JUDO MOVES
## 1 – 4

The most spectacular moves in judo are the throws. If done correctly, they allow judoka to send a much bigger attacker crashing to the ground.

### 1 Uki Goshi

*Uki goshi* was one of the favorite throws of Jigoro Kano, the founder of judo. It is a "hip throw"—one where the attacker is thrown over the defender's hip. *Uki goshi* is very useful in self-defense.

2. Blue leans forward while holding onto white and breaks her balance. This lifts white over blue's hip.

3. Blue continues to pull and twist. White is thrown over blue's hip to the floor.

1. Twisting around, the defender (blue) pulls the attacker (white) forward. Blue places her right foot between white's feet.

**2  Ippon Seoi Nage**

*Ippon seoi nage* (the one-arm shoulder throw) uses only one arm to throw an attacker over the defender's shoulder. This can take attackers by surprise, but it does require perfect timing.

**3  Eri Seoi Nage**

*Eri seoi nage* (the lapel shoulder throw) is one of the first throws new judoka learn.

**4  Morote Seoi Nage**

*Morote seoi nage* (the two-handed shoulder throw) is a spectacular throw, where the attacker is thrown right over the defender's shoulder. Like all judo throws, it requires speed and timing to be performed well.

# THE SPREAD OF JUDO

Judo soon began to become popular outside Japan as Japanese experts gave demonstrations around the world.

### Fighting the Apaches

When judo first appeared in Europe, muggers called "apaches" had begun to haunt the streets of Paris. They lay in wait for wealthy people, beat them up, and then stole their money. Judo was seen as a great way to defend against such attacks.

*The cover of this French journal from 1905 shows police officers practicing judo. Confusingly, judo was often called ju-jitsu in Europe at this time.*

## Vaudeville Judo

In the early 1900s, Japanese judo experts traveled to Europe and North and South America to give demonstrations. They appeared in vaudeville theaters and circuses, and gave demonstrations to groups of wealthy men. Soon, judo clubs sprang up wherever the Japanese had been.

*Anton Geesink of The Netherlands throws D. A. Petheridge of Great Britain. Geesink was the first non-Japanese judoka to win Olympic gold, in 1964. His success helped make judo more popular around the world.*

## INCREASING POPULARITY

As the twentieth century went on, judo became increasingly popular. Soldiers stationed in Japan after World War II (1939–45) saw judo in action and took some of its techniques home with them. Then judo appeared at the 1964 Tokyo Olympics. A movie showing the action was broadcast around the world.

# RESPECT AND DISCIPLINE

There is a well-known saying in judo: "There are only two rules in training: 1) The teacher is always right; 2) If in doubt, refer to rule 1."

## Respect

All judoka are expected to listen to their teachers carefully, and to obey their instructions without question. They must also show respect to their fellow judoka. Even away from the practice hall, judoka must behave in a way that reflects honor on their sport.

"Before and after practicing judo... opponents bow to each other. Bowing is an expression of gratitude and respect. In effect, you are thanking your opponent for giving you the opportunity to improve your technique."

*Jigoro Kano.*

## Discipline

Judoka are expected to show great discipline in their training by:

* never missing training without a good reason
* always training hard
* continuing without complaint, even when things get tough.

There's an old saying that sums this up: "When you fall down seven times, get up eight times."

In the judo movie Sanshiro Sugata, *the hero spends the night in a freezing pond to show his discipline.*

"I only train on days ending in a 'y'."

*Neil Ohlenkamp, a well-known judo instructor.*

# TOP 10 JUDO MOVES
## 5 – 7

Reaps and sweeps are fast moves that can sweep attackers off their feet before they realize what's happening.

### 5 Ouchi Gari

*Ouchi gari* (the large inner reap) is useful for self-defense. It is a good way for someone to throw an attacker who is holding on.

1. The defender (white) grips the attacker's (blue) lapel and sleeve, then pushes her shoulder with the right hand and pulls on her other arm. This puts blue off balance. White's right leg is placed behind blue's left foot, and the foot slides back along the floor. Blue's leg is hooked by the heel.

2. White brings in her back leg, then sweeps blue's foot out from under her. Blue falls backward to the ground.

## 6  Harai Goshi

*Harai goshi* (the hip sweep) is a sweep that looks very much like a throw. It is a sweep because the attacker's legs are swept out from under her as the defender pivots around to throw the attacker over her hip.

## 7  Morote Gari

*Morote gari* (the two-handed reap) is a surprise-attack move in judo. It is popular with judoka from countries where wrestling is a traditional sport. The defender uses his arms to grip the attacker's legs, and his shoulder to push the attacker over backward.

# MODERN JUDO

Today, judo is popular around the world and there are judo clubs on every continent except Antarctica. Some people even claim that worldwide, it is the second most popular sport after soccer.

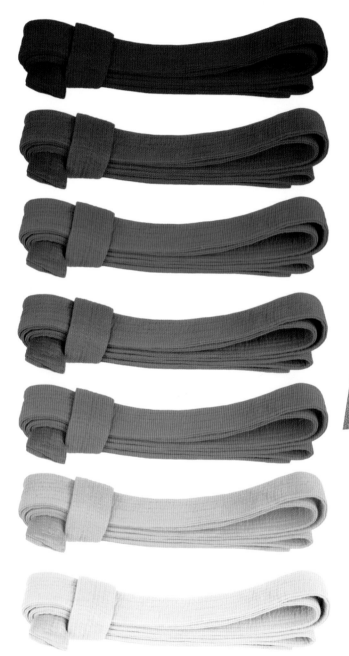

## The Belt System

Most young judoka dream of one day being a black belt. First, though, they have to work their way up through the grades. A black belt can be worn only by the very best judoka.

## BELT COLORS

As young judoka improve, they are allowed to wear different-colored belts. The colors used to show their progress are different in various parts of the world.

## Better Than Black

Black belt is not actually the top grade in judo. At the sixteenth grade, judoka can wear a red-and-white belt (or stay with black). At the nineteenth grade, they can wear red (or black).

## Judo Hits Hollywood

The first Hollywood movie featuring judo was probably the 1945 movie, *Blood On The Sun*. James Cagney—a judo black belt in real life—played a reporter who uses judo in his showdown with the movie's bad guy.

James Cagney (center, left) stars in Blood on the Sun, *a movie in which he uses judo techniques to defeat his opponents.*

"To me, judo is like ballet. Except there's no music...and the dancers knock each other down."

*Jack Handey, U.S. comedian.*

# CLUBS AND DOJOS

The very first judo club, the Kodokan, was founded in Tokyo in 1882. It used a space rented from a Buddhist monastery.

## Dojo

A *dojo* is a place where judo is taught and practiced. Today, almost every city in the world has at least one *dojo*. In places where judo is popular, there is often a choice of *dojo*.

*In judo, free practice with another judoka is called* randori. Randori *is the training that is most like actual contests.*

## Learning Safely

A *dojo* is the only place to learn judo safely. Students are grouped according to their experience and size. They learn from more experienced judoka. Some of the biggest names in judo have their own *dojo*. This means some beginners even find themselves being taught throws by world champions.

## Tatami

Judo is practiced on soft mats, to prevent judoka from being hurt when they are thrown. The mats are called *tatami*.

*Students learn in different groups. Which group they join depends on how good they are at judo.*

"I started judo with my brother when I was seven years old. I liked judo so much that I entered local tournaments, and I have a very fond memory of my first trophy."

*Laetitia Casta, top French model.*

# JUDO COMPETITION

Competitions have been an important part of judo ever since 1886, when a contest with a rival martial arts school took place (judo won!).

## Early Competitions

Early judo competitions were for men only. The rules had not yet been fully developed, and contests could be violent. Broken limbs, and even deaths, sometimes occurred.

*Competitions help judoka to improve their skills. Craig Fallon (blue) is one of the world's best young judoka. He won the 2003 World Championships silver medal.*

## Competitions Today

Today, judo's rules are designed to stop judoka from being hurt. Competitors can submit by banging on the *tatami*, or the referee can stop the bout. The winner is decided using a scoring system:

* *Ippon* is the highest score and wins the contest.
* *Waza-ari* beats all scores but *ippon*.
* *Yuko* is less than *waza-ari* and *ippon*.
* *Koka* is the lowest score.

Petersen (Denmark) has scored a *waza-ari* and been given a *koka* as a penalty against Schmidt (Germany). The "P" shows the penalty.

## Women's Competitions

Women have been involved in judo almost from the start. However, it took almost 100 years for them to become involved in competitions. The first women's World Championships took place in 1980. Women's judo first appeared at the Olympics in 1988.

"If you really want to know true judo, take a look at the methods they use at the Kodokan *joshi bu* [the women's section of Kano's judo school]."

*Jigoro Kano.*

# OLYMPIC JUDO

Judo first appeared at the Olympic Games in 1964, when they were held in Tokyo, Japan.

### Early Modern Olympics

Jigoro Kano, the founder of judo, was the first Asian member of the International Olympic Committee. Kano joined in 1909 and helped to establish the ideals of the modern Olympics.

### Famous Bouts

At every Olympics there are surprise winners and losers. The most famous Olympic bouts include

* Anton Geesink's victory over Kaminaga Akio of Japan in 1964
* David Douillet's wins in 1996 and 2000. He won the 2000 gold, although some people thought there was a judging mistake

Douillet (white) fights Shinohara (blue) at the 2000 Sydney Olympics. Many people thought that Shinohara had won the bout, but Douillet took gold.

✴ Ryoko Tamura's victory in 2004. Tamura and David Douillet were the first judoka ever to win two Olympic gold medals in a row.

*Ryoko Tamura (right) won the judo World Championships seven times and Olympic gold twice. A character in the Japanese manga Yawara is based on her.*

# TOP 10 JUDO MOVES 8—10

"Groundwork" is what happens once an opponent is on the floor. Many of judo's most dangerous moves are part of groundwork. They include strangleholds, arm locks, and leg locks.

**Competition Groundwork**

Judoka can win *ippon* using groundwork, by holding down their opponent for 25 seconds. Hold-downs for less time earn lower scores.

## 8 Kesa Gatame

*Kesa gatame* is also called the scarf hold. It gets this name from the way the competitor wraps her arm around her opponent's neck, like a scarf. At the same time, she presses her weight down on her opponent's chest and pushes her shoulders to the floor. This is very tricky to escape from!

## 9 Tate Shiho Gatame

*Tate shiho gatame* (the astride seating hold) is a way of pinning an opponent to the floor when face-to-face. It wraps the opponent up tightly, making it almost impossible for him or her to attack or escape.

## 10 The Bridge

The bridge is the most popular way of escaping a hold-down in competition. By pushing down on her heels and lifting her hips in the air, this competitor loses contact with the floor. The 25-second countdown stops, then starts at the beginning if her back touches the floor again.

# FAMOUS JUDOKA

There are many famous judoka. Some are well known within the world of judo; others are famous not only for their judo, but for other things too.

## Top-Level Judoka

The two most successful judoka of modern times are Ingrid Berghmans of Belgium and Ryoko Tamura of Japan. During the 1980s, Berghmans won a record six world titles, as well as winning the demonstration tournament at the 1988 Olympics. Tamura went one better, winning seven world titles and two Olympic golds.

*Ingrid Berghmans (rear) grapples with Isabelle Pasque of France during the semifinal of the World Championships in 1987.*

## JUDO ON SCREEN

Many actors have used judo moves on screen:
* Mel Gibson in the *Lethal Weapon* movies
* Geena Davis in *The Long Kiss Goodnight*
* Louis Koo in *Yau doh lung fu bong* (*Throw Down*)
* Bruce Willis in the *Die Hard* movies.

> "I remember one time he kicked me really hard. I remember thinking it was a good thing he only wore a size 6 shoe instead of a 14 like me, otherwise that kick would have sent me to China!"
>
> *"Judo Gene" LeBell on fighting against the martial-arts legend and close friend Bruce Lee.*

## Judo Movie Stars

Lots of martial-arts movie stars have trained in judo. Some, such as Bruce Lee (1940–73), are better known for other kinds of martial art but still practiced judo. Another judo-trained actor is Chuck Norris.

Many actors rely on stunt doubles to perform their moves. "Judo Gene" LeBell was a famous Hollywood stuntman, and judo and wrestling champion. When he won the wrestling title, LeBell was so excited that he swung his heavy winner's belt around, whacking an official with it!

*Both Bruce Lee (right) and Chuck Norris (left) went on to develop their own martial arts styles, based on all the techniques they had learned.*

# GLOSSARY

**black belt**
One of the top grades in judo, usually reached after years of practice. Although there are higher belt colors, top judoka can choose to continue wearing black even when they reach a higher grade.

**bout**
A contest, usually a fight, between two people. The word is used in many martial arts, not only in judo.

**dojo**
A place where judo is practiced and contests take place.

**grades**
Levels of achievement. Judoka usually move to a new grade at a grading exam, where they have to demonstrate their techniques and knowledge.

**ideals**
Principles or ideas that people aim to achieve. For example, one of the ideals of judo is respect for your fellow judoka.

**judoka**
People who take part in judo. *Ka* is a Japanese word that usually describes a person who is an expert at a particular activity.

**ju-jitsu**
A form of Japanese self-defense.

**kuzushi**
The skill of breaking an opponent's balance in judo. Once a person is off-balance, they are much easier to throw.

**lapel**
The front collar of a coat or jacket.

**limbs**
Arms and legs.

**manga**
Japanese comics.

**reporter**
A person who works for a newspaper, writing articles that report what is happening, also called a journalist.

**stunt double**
An athletic actor who stands in for a more famous actor in dangerous situations or fight scenes.

**submit**
To give up during a bout by banging on the mat—also called "tapping out."

**technique**
A way of doing something.

**ukemi**
Techniques for falling safely to the floor when thrown during judo.

# FURTHER INFORMATION

## BOOKS
There are many instruction books about judo, where you can learn more about some of the techniques described in this book. The only way to really learn, though, is to join a judo club.

### Judo: The Essential Guide To Mastering The Art
Alex Butcher (New Holland 2002)
Not especially aimed at younger readers, but this book has excellent step-by-step photos, and advice on training for beginners.

### Starting Sport: Judo
Rebecca Hunter (Franklin Watts, 2006)
Aimed at young people interested in learning more about judo.

### Know Your Sport: Judo
Paul Mason (Franklin Watts, 2007)
Aimed specifically at young people, this book has excellent step-by-step technique photos, plus information about what it is like to enter competitions.

## MOVIES
There are lots of movies where the stars use judo techniques, ranging from the *Lethal Weapon* series to the Sophia Loren movie, *The Millionairess*. Fewer movies are actually about judo. Some here are not suitable for all ages.

### Sanshiro Sugata (Akira Kurosawa, 1943)
The first movie ever directed by Japan's most famous filmmaker, Akira Kurosawa. *Sanshiro Sugata* tells the story of a young man who wants to become a great judoka.

### Blood on the Sun (Frank Lloyd, 1945)
Set in Japan, this movie features a young James Cagney, who was genuinely a judo black belt, chopping and throwing his way through a plot to attack the United States.

### Yau doh lung fu bong (Throw Down)
(Johnnie To, 2004)
This Chinese movie tells the story of a retired judo expert, who is challenged to a bout by a younger fighter who wants to gain fame by beating the old champion.

## WEB SITES
### www.ijf.org
The web site of the International Judo Federation, this has all sorts of interesting snippets if you dig around in the "Judo Corner" section, plus information on techniques, judo stars, world rankings, results, the history of judo, and plenty more.

### www.judoinfo.com
A general-interest site dealing with all aspects of judo, including training, techniques, frequently asked questions, and even judo jokes (most of which aren't very funny, for example, "Why is the skeleton afraid to do breakfalls?" "Because he doesn't have any guts!"), but it can tell you where to find a judo club in your state.

### www.judophotos.com
This site contains judo photos, news, features on famous judoka from Putin to Yasuhiro Yamashita, and much more.

### www.usjudo.org/
National Governing Body for Judo in the U.S.A.

Every effort has been made by the Publishers to ensure that these web sites contain no inappropriate or offensive material. However, because of the nature of the Internet, it is impossible to guarantee that the contents of these sites will not be altered. We strongly advise that Internet access is supervised by a responsible adult.

# INDEX